TREASURE ISLAND DREAMS

POEMS

by
ROGER AUBREY

Copyright © Roger Aubrey 2024

All rights reserved

No part to be reproduced without the permission of the author

Published by Lulu
ISBN 978-14461-2034-7

For Ian and David

Contents

Hispaniola
Phone Call
Joe
In Bergamo Cathedral
Three Words
Beverage
My Mother's Coat
The Man Who Knew Too Much
Present and Correct
unremarkable
The Way of Things
Coronation
The Depth of His Dying
The Reason Why
When I Was Seven
Letter to Lennon
Oldie's Ode to Summer
Thoughts and Prayers
Standoff in The Hayes
Polaroid
A Sign Spoken Against
Colours
My New Black Suit
Reverie
Food for Thought

Daily Blessing
Moment
Reflection
Tributes
Coffee and Bagels
19th September 1976
My Father's Son
Fisherman's Tale
Lessons in Love
Water-Wind
Tequila
Bartimaeus
Winter Solstice 2023
A Contemplation
Cerdinen
Rag and Bone Memories
Queen Street Paradox
Death in the Afternoon
The House of Fun
Uncle Ern
Day in the Life
Job Description
Fruit and Nut
Emmanuel
Before the Storm
The Clown

Hispaniola

I'm having Treasure Island dreams again;
and Famous Five adventures in my head.
Running through graveyards past the serried dead.
Not time to lay me there; not now, not yet.
Don't tell me to act my age; I'm younger
than I used to be. So, which age to act?
An old man in a rocking chair? A young
boy racing out the front door into the
undiscovered world beyond his opened
mind? I accept I am both these people:
a curious, wide-eyed wanderer with
wonky knees and a bus pass. Who am I?
I am Jim Hawkins on beta blockers.
Come on Timmy: we're going to Kirrin.

Phone Call

She ended the call with 'thank you'.
Stood for a moment; closed her eyes.
Opening them slowly, she walked
into the kitchen. I followed.
'Let's have a cup of tea', she said.
I put the kettle on. Waited.

She passed the milk and mugs over;
her hand rested softly on mine.
She looked out across the garden
and whispered, 'everything is fine'.

Joe

Joe sits at the bar awhile most nights,
listening through whisky ears.
Heard all their stories down the years:
dreams and plans; jokes and tears.
Courage downed; sorrows drowned.
Joe makes no sound;
just 'The usual, please,' as he plants himself down.
A small single malt;
no water, no ice.

Once they were five.
Cancer took Fred.
Bill dropped dead; his heart gave out.
Sid went in his sleep - old age, the doctor said.
Don fell down the stairs on his way up to bed.
That left Joe: alone alive.

He toasts his friends as he raises his glass.
Silently recites their names as they pass before him.
The whisky warms his body
as their memory warms his soul.

Time to go home - Daisy is waiting;
she's made toad-in-the-hole.
He smiles, recalling her silly joke about frogs and toads.
Walking to the bus his pace quickens; he's hungry -
and Daisy is waiting.

Daisy.
She knows he needs to toast his absent friends.
Joe loves Daisy. He smiles again.

In Bergamo Cathedral

She stands statue-still before the
cardinal-red rope guarding
The Holy Presence.

She is old: pure white hair,
stooping of the years, black walking stick.
Her thin frame is wrapped in
 skinny jeans, tailored jacket,
dazzling white Adidas trainers.

I think mutton and lamb.
Ignorant, judgemental iconoclast
I still sometimes am.
She is dignified, reverent.
Dressed in her best to worship her God.
And Italian:
stylish even in matters of religion.

She stares above the opulent, ornate altar,
laden with chalices, candles, paraphernalia
beyond my Protestant understanding.
I follow her gaze to a small black wooden cross;
a gold Christ impaled on it.
I gaze.

A stentorian pronouncement from my past disturbs me:
'No crucifixes here. He is not dead. He has risen.'

Slowly she moves away, heavy on her stick,
to a small side chapel, dedicated:
CHRISTUM REGEM VENITE ADOREMUS

Quiet and brown-dark.
Against the gloom the spotlit
Crucifixed Christ dies in glorious public agony.
She sits to one side, halfway back,
rosary rotating through arthritic fingers.
Tourists make media moments.
My camera remains in the bag,
reluctant to desecrate her
Most Holy Place.

    Behold
CHRISTUM REGEM

As I leave, I pass a font.
Cross myself with sacred water.

Three Words

I watched him die. My beloved brother.
His life snuffed out so quickly. On Monday
he was fine. Tuesday the fever hit him;
by Thursday night he was fighting for breath.
Early Friday morning he was gone. Cold.
Now he's sitting across the room from me,
eating his breakfast. He has the strangest
look on his face: bewildered confusion.
I guess four days dead will do that to you.
Three words shouted - and there he was: in his
grave wraps, shuffling out with slow, baby steps.
I had words with my friend just before he
called out to my dead brother. 'You're too late',
I said. 'I am Resurrection', he said.

Beverage

I know I'm not your
cup of tea.
I could be your
cappuccino.

My Mother's Coat

The day my brother and I crossed a line.
'That's it. I've had enough of you two.'
'I'm leaving.'
My brother cried and pleaded with mum to stay.

I fetched her coat.
The black Sunday-best one she liked the most.
'Here you are mum. 'Bye.'
She aimed a slap at the back of my head;
the slap she'd greet me with when I'd played with the gang.
'That's for everything God saw you do,' she would intone from
her kitchen pulpit.

I didn't like God:
The All-Seeing Informer
in league with
The All-Powerful Matriarch.
They presented a formidable challenge to a nine year old
set on having fun, risking their killjoy gaze.
They wouldn't ruin my long summer days.

I put the Dynamic Duo to the test,
baby step offences at first:
a drag on dad's ciggy, left on his workbench in the shed;
forgetting my prayers when I went up to bed.

Nothing.

Bigger and braver contraventions followed
(modesty forbids…)
God's hand stayed at mum's side.
I was on my way, ready to ride into my teens.

Mum didn't put the coat on;
she went into the bathroom, came out a while later and
hung it back up.
Years later she told me: 'I had to go and laugh at what
you'd said and done.'
She never again threatened to leave her two sons.

The Man Who Knew Too Much

He was one to gladly cast the first stone.
He had a degree in finger pointing;
a PhD in shooting from the hip.
He had a nickname: they called him The Lip.
He delighted in putting people right.
He knew where all the bodies were buried
and what happened in Dallas '63.
Colleagues' eyes glazed over when he started
his latest diatribe: appointments were
remembered; excuses made: 'Late for tea'.
He lived alone. Mary left years ago,
worn down by his irrefutable truth.
He missed having her to talk at. He bought
a cat and talked to it. It slept a lot.

Present and Correct

I bought your books today
in the hospice charity shop.
Poets of the Great War: Faber and Faber Collection.
Owen. Thomas. Brooke. Sassoon. Jones. Graves.
Still in the cellophane.
All Present and Correct, Sir.

Original sticker price: sixty three quid - now a tenner,
down from twenty five,
gathering time-and-tide dust,
buried on a bottom shelf
at the back of the shop.

Like Abel, though dead
you speak:

The common sky is still infected
with the misery that befalls.

Doomed youth still die and
lie in foreign fields.

We never forget those
who leave alone.

From:
Recalling War (Robert Graves)
In Parenthesis (David Jones)
Anthem for Doomed Youth (Wilfred Owen)
The Soldier (Rupert Brooke)
Aftermath (Siegfried Sassoon)
Lights Out (Edward Thomas)

unremarkable

When they were apportioning blame,
he was plonked in the Circle of Shame.
When they voted Least Likely to Succeed,
he was placed in the Hall of Fame.

In the Lottery of Destiny
he drew the ticket of mediocrity;
pity his simplicity.

The Potentialists marked him out
for below-average-ness:
'Try not to make a mess
of your life.'

Filed under:
unexceptional
no great shakes
unremarkable

      he showed them

The Way of Things

You sowed the Wind;
what did you expect?
Did you forget
the Way of Things?

Learn from the Whirlwind;
when it has done its reaping,
seeds remain.
This is the Way of Things.

Coronation

A crown of mocking thorns rammed down on it.
Then the pushing, shoving, jostling, jolting;
manhandled through late night furtive 'justice'.
Hardened fists smashed the spittle spattered face;
its life blood slowly dripping on the earth.
Then the abused body was stripped naked,
pinned to the ground as iron hammered in;
hoisted high into place for all to see.
As the death throes finally consumed it,
a cold blade thrust into the quiet heart,
shuddering the body one final time.
Embedded in its skull the Crown held firm.
After all, this was a coronation;
a king crowned on a bloody, wooden throne.

The Depth of His Dying
(From Julian of Norwich)

He died deeply —
descended to death's deepest depth,
shroud-entombed in death's desolate vault
of abandoned hope.
Silence. Deep Death Silence.

———

…
…flicker of eyelid…
…flare of nostril…
…flit of finger…

The Reason Why

She never tells me why she loves me.
Never has, never will.
I ask her still:
she says, 'Just because.'

Oh, she tells me she loves me.
I know that she loves me;
as sure as eggs is eggs.
But I'm blowed if I know why she loves me.
'Just because' is all she says.

I give her reasons why I love her.
If she gave me one in return:
I put out the bins, can find anything;
do the gardening and vacuuming.
I'm always willing to learn.
She gives me just because.
Forty five years.
Just because.

When I Was Seven

'Mum, where's Random?'
'What, love?'
'Where's Random? When I grow up
I'm going to live there.'

'Random? Do you mean Rangoon?
There's no place called called Random.'

'Yes there is, and I'm
going to live there.'

'What are you talking about, love?'
'On the radio,
when there's a competition,
the man always says
the winner will be chosen at Random.
It's the luckiest place in the whole wide world!'

Letter to Lennon

Dear John,
No one read the news today.
Oh boy.

Yours,
S. Pepper

Oldie's Ode to Summer

I'm so looking forward to summer
It's the season when I look my best
Rosy red cheeks and a spring in my step
And I don't have to wear a warm vest

The shorts go on early in summer
My legs shiny white in the sun
They're still just as pale in September
But they've given the family fun

I never wear sandals in summer
Or flip flops that slip off my feet
It's deck shoes - no socks - 'cause that's how I rock
I still march to a Steve McQueen beat

We visit the seaside in summer
And paddle right up to our knees
Then pop in at Mrs Ramsbottom's
For two of her afternoon teas

We go on a coach trip in summer
With the Old Fogey Stannah lift set
But we still climb the stairs just to show them
There's life in the old greyhounds yet

I love a cold cider in summer
Sometimes it goes straight to my head
My wife says I drink it too quickly
So I sip a Prosecco instead

I like watching cricket in summer
The village game's perfect for me
A warm afternoon in a deckchair
A snooze and a nice cup of tea

I enjoy my old garden in summer
Hydrangeas and fuchsias galore
I'm grateful they made it through winter
We'll be flowering for many years more

I wake very early in summer
And walk in the cool of the day
I give thanks to God for my family and friends
For my health and for guiding my way

I love the long evenings of summer
The temperature reaching its peak
I'm so looking forward to summer
They say it's on Wednesday next week

Thoughts and Prayers

Thoughts and prayers are with the families.
Your heart-felt sincerity must be of immense comfort
as they bury their stabbed and bullet-ridden kids.
When they hear how their loved ones suffocated in
the back of an abandoned lorry.
When the public enquiry reveals the extent of
neglect and abuse.
When they're flooded out of their homes again.
When their village is reduced to ashes.
After the earthquake's final tremor.

To whom do you pray?
What and why do you pray?
What are your thoughts?
How do they reach the families?
What difference do they make?

Don't say
'Lessons will be learned.'
You'll only be repeating yourself next time.

Standoff in The Hayes

Leaving Waterstones with
Billy Collins in the bag,
a chopsy, spotty Big Issue seller
with a German Shepherd
stops me:

'Any spare change, mate?'
I give him a quid; he winks —
'One more, so I can get a good coffee?'
I smile, oblige. He smiles, grateful.
'Cheers, mate' — scurries off with the mutt,
passing an older man coming my way with a
Heinz '57 mongrel.

He must have seen our transaction;
taken exception to Chopsy,
shouts abuse at him.
Clearly they have previous;
start on at each other,
Cardiff boys doing their city proud.

I'm on my way;
I don't have a dog in this fight.
The ugly noise of escalating verbals follows me
past the Market into St John's Square.

I turn into Queen Street;
back in The Hayes
they're still going hammer and tongs,
Chopsy edging it in the
decibel stakes,
Mongrel Man in insults.

It's not every day
kindness starts
World War Three.

Polaroid

In the comfort and the pain of darkness,
I sit and wonder: what became of us?
When did our everlasting light go out?
When did it start its final flickering?
Did we talk for years and yet say nothing?
Was it that chat you had with your sister?
Or did you never get over Robert?
Did we become so used to each other
that I got to the end of you and you
got to the end of me? I wish, I wish
I'd thought to ask us a long time ago.
The glow of my cigarette falls on a
photo; I found it last night in a drawer.
My heart skipped a beat. What became of us?

A Sign Spoken Against

He began well.
People liked him, even though we didn't get
what he was on about some of the time.
He often freaked us out:
flying pigs off cliffs;
rubbing mud in blind people's eyes;
pulling cash from a fish's mouth;
hugging lepers (that was gross).
Still, there was something good about him.

God knows why:
he decided to take on the Big Boys.
Went out of his way to put their backs up:
doing unholy stuff on their holy days;
bamboozling their brains;
speaking his truth to their power.
What really riled them was how he
opposed their teaching of The Book.
Talk about red rag to a bull;
risking life and limb.

He got personal.
Called them hypocrites, swindlers, liars.
Said their mouths were stinking, open graves.
The lot of them rotten to the core.

The straw that broke the camel's back
came when he dubbed them
sons of the devil.
To their faces.

We knew from that moment he was a
dead man walking.
It was only a matter of time:
they'd crush him like a bug under their feet.

Strange: it was like he had a death wish.

Colours

I met a man going nowhere.
He said, 'Come nowhere with me.'
He knew a girl who had her own umbrella;
she tried to sell me the weather.

They knew a woman who owned a rainbow:
 seven shades of black.
I asked her for the colours in her sack;
she gave me green and blue.
They reminded me of you.

My New Black Suit

I've bought a new black suit: M&S relaxed fit.
Making good use of it:
two weddings, three funerals.
Hoping it will last a bit.

Don't bury me in my black suit; this is my decree:
Give my body to the medics so they can learn from me.
Much better that than to bury or burn me.
Don't you agree?
Good to be useful one last time.
Don't waste your money:
I'll be just fine.

Give my suit to the British Heart Foundation
as a suitable token of appreciation.
Or stick it in a charity bag
that comes through the door.
I'm not that fussed:
I won't need it anymore.

Reverie

Winter afternoon by an open fire.
Listen to the hallelujah choir.
Call to mind forgotten places,
Half remembered names and faces.
Move in closer as the welcome flames burn higher.

Easing in the warm and restful room;
Eyes adjusting to the gathering gloom.
An ancient ticking clock becalms my mind;
Leave the hustle bustle far behind.
Await the rising of the crescent moon.

Eyes grow heavy, feel the need for sleep.
Breathing softens, gentle, slow and deep.
Senses rising up from far below;
Images in sepia come and go.
A chasm opens up, ink black and steep.

Travelling through corridors of time;
Drifting past a home that once was mine.
The door is open wide,
I pause to look inside;
She stands alone in half-light speaking rhymes.

Hair still long, now ageing into grey;
Her eyes, still kind and blue, now look away.
She reaches out her hand;
In her smile I understand.
Recites her Psalm and then begins to pray.

Peering in the flames I see a face:
A childhood friend whose name has been erased.
Recall that he was brave;
I visited his grave.
The stone calls him 'an angel filled with grace.'

In the shadows stands a stooping, shrouded man;
Strokes his chin with a gnarled, familiar hand.
I stare, but cannot see:
My father, brother - me?
He slowly sinks beneath the shifting sand.

On a table lies a well-worn Ancient Book.
It beckons me to take a closer look.
Drink deep and long of its transforming power,
The ancient clock chimes out the passing hours.
Returns me to a path that I once took.

A strange sensation washes over me,
A Holy Presence that my heart can see.
It whispers in my ear
Secrets I've longed to hear.
A fire burns in my blood and I am free.

A drowsing sweet aroma fills the room,
Like incense in a saint's well-treasured tomb.
The fire is burning low;
And in the dying glow
I lose all sense of hopelessness and doom.

An angel hand lays wood upon the fire.
The crackling sound it makes awakes the choir.
Their faces my old friends
Who loved me to their end.
Their mystic music lifts my spirit higher.

A melancholy sighing fills the air;
It settles like a cloak around my chair.
It wraps me in its sound;
It murmurs, 'You are found.'
I fall asleep while offering a prayer.

Awake. The room is dark; a winter night.
The crescent moon appears; it shares its light.
I think of all I've seen;
What was or might have been.
I shiver in the cold that grips me tight.

Food For Thought

Yesterday was an utter donkey's breakfast;
today was a complete dog's dinner.
I wonder what's for lunch tomorrow?

Daily Blessing

He scurries towards me, emerging from the mist
like a compact holy ghost,
slight stoop of the pit-life, flat cap perched
at an angle he likes to call jaunty.
Off to the corner shop for the paper.

'Morning, my boy' —
seven or seventy, you're 'my boy.'
'Morning Mr Evans, how are you today?'
His answer's always the same:
'As He is, my boy, as He is.
God bless you, my boy, God bless you.'

His blue-scarred hand gently
taps my shoulder as he passes,
and I am blessed.

Moment

This new day
gives you another chance
to
make a fresh start.
If the hours ahead bring sadness
and good news is
nil,
remember that moment
she kissed you.

Reflection

I thought that
life would turn out better
than
it has become.
We could have sung a sweeter song;
found kinder words
to
wipe away the sadness
in our eyes.

Tributes

We all came out for Carla today.
Paid our respects, honoured her memory,
showed our faces for the family,
commiserated, celebrated,
caught up with friends.

We wore our best black -
except for Gary and Sally,
who looked liked
they'd flown in from Benidorm
(they drove from Hull.)

Carla left instructions:
not too long and don't be boring.
Credit to her: it was an Ecclesiastes occasion -
a time to weep, a time to laugh.

Exit via the family lineup:
wonderful service; sorry for your loss;
look after yourself; praying for you;
anything you need; get together soon.

It always reminds me of the Queen
meeting the teams at the Cup Final -
only she just smiled.

Why do we save our tributes for funerals?
Carla didn't hear a word.
I suppose they're for our sake, part of the process.

We could pour our tributes in while
they're alive.
Mind you: Carla would probably
die of embarrassment.

Coffee and Bagels

I got up early to meet you;
you were already waiting for me.
I needed coffee; you were raring to go.
I sipped my way into your day,
congratulated you on the creation of the arabica bean.

Settling into my sacred chair -
cushions exactly how I'd left them -
I watched the robins, sparrows, blue and coal tits, dunnocks,
blackbirds, and a solitary pigeon, enjoying their
communal breakfast on the move, one eye watching out
for cats and magpies. I slowly chewed a bagel,
pondering if they ever get indigestion from eating so fast.

I remembered what you said about
the Father feeding them;
but thought, '*I* bought the seed, suet balls, the feeders
and the table.' *I* was feeding them.
You said, 'But who gave you seed to buy the seed?'

I found the place in my Bible where you talked about
birds and barns, flowers and Solomon, coffee and bagels,
(or whatever they had for breakfast in those days).
And not to worry about stuff because
'Your heavenly Father knows what you need.'

Naturally, my mind went to
this morning's appointment;
I decided it would go OK.
I had another coffee and jumped in the shower.
The birds kept munching away.

19th September 1976

I went to dad's greenhouse the morning he died,
cocooned myself in his final summer.
It was Sunday; he should have been in church.
He lay stroke-comatose in hospital, mum holding his hand,
waiting for his angels.

I cwtched in a corner, face buried in his gloves,
his tomato plants my canopy, their fruit blood-red ripe.
We were supposed to pick them that afternoon.

Shock stopped up the tears.
Numb. Prayed. Nauseous.
Clashing clattering chaotic thoughts.
Reality loomed.
Waited…

Just before noon my brother's feet crunched the gravel path,
heralding the end - and a beginning.
We sat shoulder to shoulder in our silent sanctuary.
I took dad's gloves with me.

I returned to the greenhouse two months later - my birthday.
A cold, stale smell, fruit withered, plants shrivelled dirty brown.
I ripped them out; threw them on the compost heap.
They'd return to feed a crop I never grew.

My Father's Son

I still hold the door open for ladies of all ages or an older man
(even though I'm seventy one). Help folks on with their coats.
Doff my cap. Stand up when a lady first enters the room. Offer
my seat on the bus if they're pregnant,
herding their kids or look like they need a sit down.
Sometimes just to be kind.

Last week a pleasant young girl said to me 'Please take my seat
sir' - I was thrilled by her care and manners - and shocked - do
I look that old?
I thanked her for her offer and politely declined:
stood straighter and held on a little bit tighter.
The first time anyone has done that for me.

I look people in the eye as I firmly shake their hand. Smile.
Say 'please' and 'thank you, you're welcome, after you, God
bless you.'
Clean the backs of my shoes. Carry a fresh cotton hanky.
Keep my powder dry and my fingernails clipped and clean.
Never raise my voice or hand to Dianne —
or any woman for that matter.

Don't drop litter. Say, 'Spoken like a proper twerp'
when I disagree with someone on the TV (far too often these
days).

Can't sit still when Wales play England. Don't curse or swear.
Bang my bald head on things.

Tell my grandsons (twelve and seven),
'Boys, manners maketh the man.'
Their dad (forty) agrees: 'Poppy is right.'
My father lives on; I am Ray Aubrey's boy.

Fisherman's Tale

For those few, brief moments
he was King of the Hill.
Calloused feet striding out on churning sea.
A foolhardy request.
An open hand beckoning.
And he was over the side into a new world.

Of course, he began to sink.
It's not where we belong.
We belong in boats, bottoms glued to seats.
Laugh at him - another self inflicted disaster.
But for those few, brief - glorious - moments
he went boldly where only One had gone before.

Lessons in Love

Love sneaks up when you least want it to;
Shouts 'BOO!'
And scares you to death.
Love creeps up on you, covers your eyes,
Murmurs, 'Guess who' under its breath.

Love is untamed and raw;
Love socks you square on the jaw;
Stays put when you show it the door.
Love nails itself to the floor.

Love is violent: it mows down hate.
Love slams its heart flat down on your plate.
Love sings out loud at the top of its voice;
Love tells you straight not to make that dumb choice.
Love makes it clear: 'there's no reason to fear.'
Love loves incessantly, year after year.

Love is a pest; love always says yes
To the one who always says no.
Love ruffles your hair;
Love jumps in your chair;
Love says, 'I won't let you go.'

Love has no shame,
Love's a brazen hot flame.
Love gets in your face
When you're quitting your race.
Love makes a mess all over the place.
Love is an utter disgrace.

Water-Wind

Water-Wind flowing-blowing
in iridescent power,
seeking inner sanctums of eternal souls,
awaking, reviving long ago songs
of angels who wept at the
dragon's tail-sweep.

Subway prophets seek new walls,
their wisdom erased in the angst graffiti
of those who spray their prayers.

In the death-deep plastic ocean
Atlantis hides, awaiting the
Manifest Sons.

Blind tell deaf what they see.
Deaf sign blind what they hear.
Mute - I watch, listen;
wait for
Water-Wind.

Tequila

You say you've not decided yet.
Really?
Emma is perfect - she's the one for you.
Let yourself go. I know you want to.
You know you need to.
Emma loves you to death;
and she's so not like Beth.

You were a spring chicken years ago;
you've said you're not sure or just don't know
way too many times.
You've been like it since school;
honestly Billy - you're being a fool.
I'm your friend so I'm telling you straight:
marry Emma before it's too late.

Her photo's the screen on your phone;
her Abba song is your family ringtone!
Your eyes lit up when you saw her today;
you miss her like crazy when she's working away.
She's put a huge grin all over your face;
you've even lost weight and tidied your place.

That thing with Beth was a long time ago.
We warned you not to go
away with her. Always bound to end in tears.

She broke your heart, ran off with Chad,
who bought you tequila so he could steal her
away from you. Just as we feared.
Beth knew tequila makes you bad;
it was she who told Chad;
he told me all this when she dumped him.
I'm glad you're free of her.

(Beth always had a thing for Americans
with cool names).

It's clear to us all you're totally smitten;
why else would you give Emma the kitten?
Remember? - you told me she is the one
the last time we were out for a run.
Plus - she hates tequila.
You know you've decided - please do the right thing:
take her shopping this weekend: buy her the ring.

Bartimaeus

Dumbest question I'd ever been asked.
Miracle man, specialising in people like me.
I knew all about him;
on these streets you hear everything,
huddled in a corner with a begging bowl.

I heard the kerfuffle - he was on the other side of the road,
leaving town. Now or never.
Gave it full blast. Luckily he heard me,
called me over. Puzzled he didn't come to me,
given my condition.

Barged my way to his voice, stumbled right into him.
Almost knocked him flying. He managed to stop us
collapsing in a heap.
He chuckled. I caught my breath.
Reckoned he was about my height,
maybe a tad taller.

'What do you want me to do for you?'

Hit me for six. Thought:
Are you serious? You having a laugh?
How I didn't blurt out a smart alec comeback,
God alone knows.

I still don't get what happened next.
His question got in my head:
if this works, what will it mean?
Discover what I look like.
Learn to read and write.
Find a place. Get a job.
A wife and kids someday?
Can I handle this?
Those few moments felt like
eternity.

He was so close I could feel his breath on my face.
(He'd been eating olives and figs).
He didn't say a word;
just waited for my answer.
'I want to see.'

Winter Solstice 2023

A sense: these long-night days are far more than
a phase I am passing through. The chill touch
of life's winter shroud on my shoulders; the
fading shadows of older friends. I turn
away from dying sun, low and west-red;
face dayspring-east, whence it will live again.
Dayspring! Risen with healing in Your wings;
eternal kingdom's never-setting Dawn.
My thorn-crowned King; my Sun of righteousness.
I see You, but not yet, Star of Jacob.
Lay me dust-low; I too will live again.
Tomorrow and farewell; the comforting
tolling of the bell. I know for whom it
tolls: It tolls for me. Yes, it tolls for me.

A Contemplation

To know that I am fully known.
To know the One who fully knows me.
To know that I will never fully know
The One who fully knows me.

To know that I am fully loved.
To love the One who fully loves me.
To love Him more fully as I know Him more fully.
To know Him more fully as I love Him more fully.
For all Eternity.

To know and love the
One who is Infinity.
This is profound simplicity.

Cerdinen

On the path to the twilight sea,
a melancholy melody calls to me,
ethereal and low,
a song of long ago.

I turn aside to see
this voice that beckons me;
it draws me to a solitary
timeworn rowan tree.

A blackbird gorges on the
Christ-blood fruit.
Cerdinen weeps;
bleak wind cuts deep;
Ancients rest in grave-sleep.

From a high branch a
mistle thrush laments:
'Who will keep
      Faith?'
'Who will keep
      Faith?'
'Who will keep
      Faith?'

Rag and Bone Memories

Every couple of weeks or so,
Big Ned
clopped slowly up our road,
pulling Tommy Badman's cart
with its growing load.

Tommy Badman -
Rag and Bone Man -
calling out low and slow -
'rag-bonio…any old iron…rag-bonio'.

Sixteen hands; tar-black; grey mane.
Solid as a stone wall, Big Ned -
soulful eyes; noble head.

Old Mrs Hart always had something
for Tommy's cart:
the leg bone from Sunday's lamb, boiled clean.
Tom would give her a few pennies more
than he paid the others;
all the mothers
understood.

Mrs Hart lost her boy Jackie in the war.
Lancaster Tail Gunner. Twenty four.

Mrs Hart was fond of Tommy;
it was mutual.
He and Jackie were friends since school.
Tommy was Royal Engineers in the war -
Far East, building Bailey Bridges.
Tommy was a good man to old Mrs Hart.
He missed Jackie; broke his heart
when he got the news.

Folks said Mrs Hart had a heart of gold.
She'd give us kids carrots for Ned.
Once I offered him a piece of bread;
Ned snorted, shook his noble head;
soulful eyes stared me down:
'Give me carrots instead.'

When Ned had done his business of the day,
and Tommy was finally on his way,
dad would shove a shovel and bag
in my hand.
'Only way to make money on a nag,'
he'd say.
'Rhubarb and roses
won't go hungry today.'

True story:
when Mrs Hart passed away
Tommy's cart carried her to her grave.
Ned held his noble head
high all the way.

Later that day
I fed Ned a carrot to say
thank you.
His soulful eyes
looked deep into mine.

Queen Street Paradox

The Witness for Jehovah
stands silent and impassive
under the statue of
the prophet Nye.

Nobody makes eye
contact with her
as they pass by.

Death in the Afternoon

Rat.
Laid out on the patio,
mauled, mangled, left for dead
by the big ginger tom
who parades through my garden
like a Mafia Don.

Feline fun in the summer sun.
Death in the afternoon
can't come too soon
for a wretched rodent

in its final shuffle;
fetch the shovel.
One sharp blow:
on its way
to where rats go.

The House of Fun

The wizened magician forgot his best trick,
The inebriated fire-eater called in sick,
The fastest gun in the west is no longer that quick,
The House of Fun is falling down brick by brick.

The elastic contortionist can no longer bend,
The brave tightrope walker's afraid to ascend,
The happy-faced clown now loves to offend,
The House of Fun is reaching the end.

The monkey ventriloquist chewed through her lip,
The old-time tap dancer has arthritic hips,
The well placed banana skin refuses to slip,
The House of Fun is losing its grip.

The one-liner comic won't joke anymore,
The light-fingered juggler drops the balls on the floor,
The white-whiskered ringmaster walked out of the door,
The House of Fun will soon be no more.

Uncle Ern

When the train reached Cogan
we could hardly contain ourselves.
The annual family outing to Barry Island,
highlight of the summer holidays,
was only one stop away.

Ten minutes later we were on the beach.
We always sat by the big 4 painted
on the sea wall:
mum's lucky number and where we'd find her
among the madding crowd.

Uncle Ern and Aunty Lil, (mum's sister),
always came with us.
They couldn't have kids so
we were kind of surrogates.
Ern was mad as a box of frogs.

Once, he decided to do a
running belly flop into the water.
He launched himself,
landed smack on his front and
disappeared beneath the waves.

A few seconds later he shot to the surface:
'Blimey, I've lost me teeth!'
We all foraged but failed to find
Ern's dentures.

Lil took the spam out of his sandwich
so he could suck the bread and butter.
Ern spent the rest of the day gurning.

Day in the Life

Today I forgot the common name
for Myosotis is forget-me-not.

Today I sang all the words
to Sgt. Pepper: the whole album.

Today I lost my mobile phone.
I found it in my pocket.

Today I fixed the new Dyson
to the wall in the garage.

Today I recalled something I knew,
but can't recollect what it was.

Today I learned to use the
back button focus on my camera.

Today I forgot the common name
for Myosotis is forget-me-not.

Job Description

Give him the name Jesus; he will save his people from their sins.

Saviour, you're causing some problems.
We're not so sure about sin anymore.
Saviour, please could you help us; tell us:
Precisely what are you for?

Fruit and Nut

Awake early.
Coffee; Wordle in three: a rarity.
Last night's dream returns to me:
chatting with Monty Don in the pub
about sweet peas
while he helped himself to my peanuts.

I excused myself and headed
for the toilet.
I never get to use the loos in my dreams;
they're down impossibly long corridors
or occupied when I find them.

My bladder alarm woke me.
Time for the one o'clock visit;
second trip came around three-thirty.
Normal in your seventies —
you have been warned.

The doctor says my once young walnut is
now an aged tangerine.
Having my workings described as food
is a wee bit disconcerting, especially
when I peel an orange or
eat a walnut whip.

Apparently, cooked tomatoes are good for tangerines.
I must ask Monty which variety he recommends.

Emmanuel

He is here
Word of God, who will one day learn his alphabet
He is here
Self-Sufficient One, needing his smelly nappy changed
He is here
Bread of Life, hungry, guzzling Mary's milk to thrive
He is here
Upholder of the universe, helpless, carried in Joseph's arms
He is here
All-Knowing God, gurgling away, blissfully ignorant and unaware
He is here
All-Powerful God, unable to raise his royal head
He is here
All-Seeing God, fast asleep on a straw-strewn bed
He is here
Holy God, dribble running down his chin
He is here
Prince of Peace, making a din with his colic
He is here
Healer of the sick, sucking his Comforting thumb
He is here
one with us; one of us
He is here

Before the Storm

They'd finally got him. Dead and buried,
done and dusted, the chaotic city
quieting down. His followers were in
hiding; they'd scuttle back up north once they
felt safe enough to break cover and make
a run for it. Let them go; they wouldn't
dare cause trouble now he was out of the
picture. Things were returning to normal.
The incident with the Temple curtain
was unfortunate; it was getting old
and should have been replaced long ago. Least
said soonest mended. Early next week it
would be sorted. But first, time for Sabbath.
Sunday dawned calm. All was well with their world.

The Clown

Sitting in the sunshine eating my daily bread.
Listening to the radio and the music in my head.
I saw a clown across the street;
He waved at me with both his feet.
He shouted at the count of three:
'The whole world's crazy, not just me.
Look for yourself and you will find
The things you see will blow your mind.'

He sang a song about the moon,
But all the words were out of tune.
The moon shone bright all day and night,
But then it disappeared from sight.
The man in the moon was smiling
Since the flying men went away;
But now he's sad 'cause he just heard
They're coming back again.

It's been a while since I was here;
Things haven't changed, that much is clear.
'The poor are rich and the rich are poor,'
So the rich man said as he grabbed for more.
'Let justice roll down like a river,'
That's what the prophet said;
But nobody was listening
As they plundered all the dead.

The water men drowned the rivers
In a sea of their own crud.
Then they charged us for the honour
Of cleaning up the flood.
They were laughing without smiling,
And they said, 'It's all OK.'
But they sacrificed our future
On the altar of their pay.

The March Hare said to Alice,
'The Joker's on his way;
Just humour him, he'll soon be gone
But he has to have his day.'
He who pays the ferryman
As he crosses Acheron;
And the one who pays the piper
Will be here before long.

Then the sandman said to Alice,
'It's time to get some sleep.'
She closed her eyes and prayed to God
For him her soul to keep.
She dreamed of endless summers
That never saw the sun;
And shivered in the cold new dawn
As she reached down for the gun.

Ulysses and the Waste Land
Made sense to me at last.
A Day in the Life of the Walrus
Went by us all too fast.
We sang 'We are the champions'
And 'All you need is love.'
We thought we'd live forever
Like the boy with the crystal glove.

The mystery of the universe
Was there for all to see;
But we wouldn't put our glasses on
We thought that we were free.
We were trapped inside our knowledge
In the smallness of our minds,
While the Maker of the heavens
Reached down and healed the blind.

The scoundrel's smooth and silky words
Ruined the helpless poor.
He promised the world and a precious pearl
As he eased them through the door.
Out in the dark they froze in the cold
As he burned their houses down.
Their days were done, they'd never grow old;
Then I looked at that old clown.

I threw a drowning man a brick
And shouted, 'That'll do the trick.'
He held it high in both his hands;
It flew him to the Promised Land.
The clown he bowed his head and cried,
He held his arms out open wide.
I said to him, 'Don't be surprised;
The ways of God will blow your mind.'

Printed in Great Britain
by Amazon